Snakes Have No Legs!

Kelly Tills

A division of FDI publishing LLC

The wonderful thing
about snakes is...

snakes have no
legs!

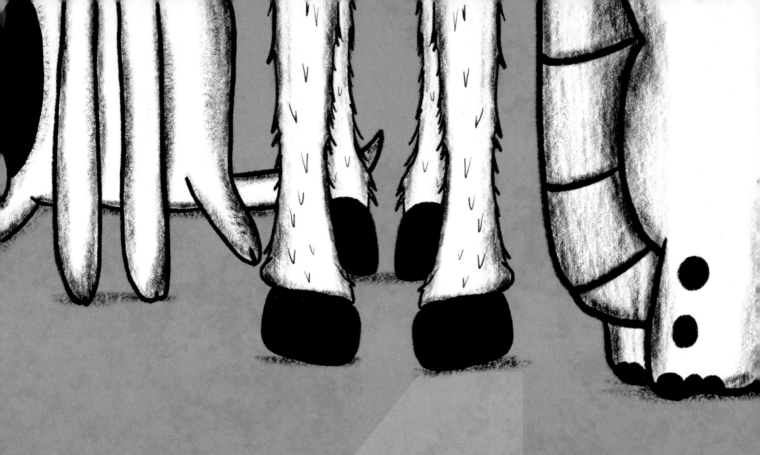

Lots of animals have four legs.

Birds have two legs.
Flamingos think they have one.

Can a snake wear shoes?

No!
They have no feet.

Can a snake wear
gloves?

No!
They have no hands.

Can a snake wear a scarf?

Well, maybe a very long one.

If snakes don't walk or run, how do they move around?

They
slither!

Snakes have lots of tiny belly muscles that wiggle up and down, and their bodies go side to side.

They can slither very fast, or very slow. They can slither on the ground, up a tree, or in the water.

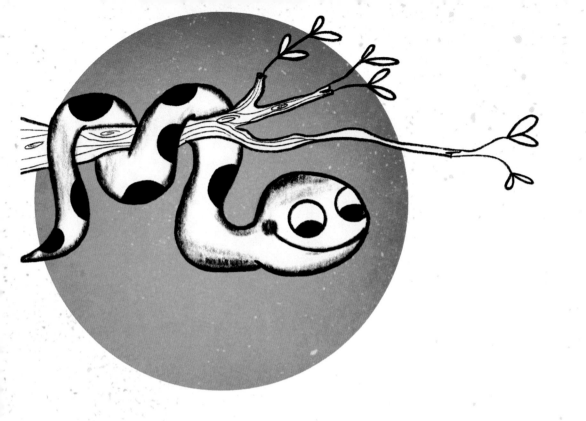

Can a snake slither in the air?

No!
They have no wings.

Can a snake slither in
space?

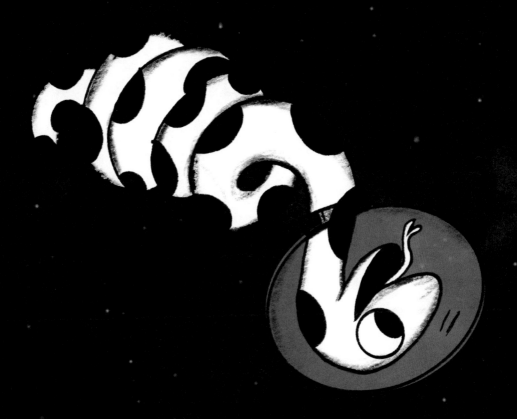

That's a silly question.

They can twist their bodies into lots of shapes,

and they can certainly
win a race!

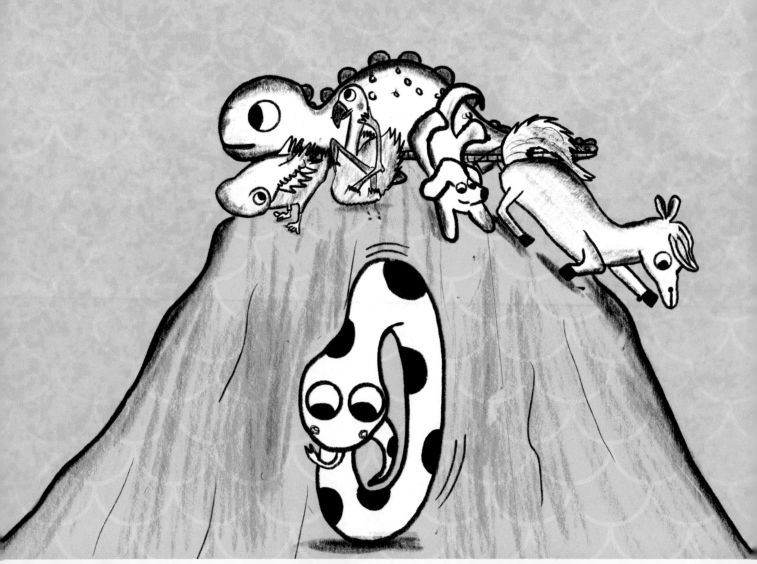

And that's the wonderful thing
about snakes.

What's the
wonderful thing
about
you?

Well, actually...

back in prehistoric times,
snakes had legs! That was over
100 million years ago.

Whoa! That's crazy.

Get More *Awesome Animals* Books

  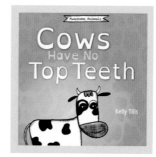 

About the Author

Kelly Tills writes silly books for kids and believes even the smallest hat-tip, in the simplest books, can teach our kids how to approach the world. Kelly's children's stories are perfect to read aloud to young children, or to let older kids read themselves (hey, let them flex those new reading skills!). Proud member of the *International Dyslexia Association*.

I hope this book brought you and your tiny human some fun time together. Help others find this book, and experience that same joy by **leaving a review!**

Point your phone's camera here.

It'll take you straight to the review page. Magic!

Made in the USA
Monee, IL
02 July 2024